8802697

j 597.9
P45r

Petty, Kate
Reptiles

OPRC   2nd Gr. 1988-89

ε ✓

© Aladdin Books Ltd

Designed and produced by
Aladdin Books Ltd
70 Old Compton Street
LONDON W1

*First published in the
United States in 1987 by*
Gloucester Press
387 Park Avenue South
New York NY 10016

ISBN 0 531 17063 2

Certain illustrations originally published in
The Closer Look Series

Reptiles

Contents

Reptiles

Kate Petty

Illustrated by
Gary Hincks, Alan Male, Phil Weare

small world

Gloucester Press
New York · London · Toronto · Sydney

What are reptiles?

Snakes, lizards, crocodiles and turtles are
all reptiles. Dinosaurs were reptiles.
They all have dry, scaly skins.
Their babies hatch from eggs.
Reptiles are not warm-blooded, like mammals.
They are cold blooded,
which means that their body temperature changes
as the air around them changes.

Crocodiles

Lizard

Snake

Turtle

7

Cold-blooded creatures
Cold-blooded creatures need sun to warm them up
and shade or water to cool them down.
Most of them live in hot countries.
These Marine iguanas jump into the sea
when the rocks become too hot.

Shade is hard to find in the desert.
Some desert reptiles, like this Sidewinder
rattlesnake, bury themselves in the sand.
The Sidewinder disappears from sight
very quickly.

Reptile babies
Female snakes and lizards produce their eggs
from an opening called the cloaca.
Some snakes and lizards hatch while they are
still inside the mother and are born live.
A tiny "egg tooth" helps the snake come out
of its egg. A snake can look after itself right away.

An Indigo snake laying eggs

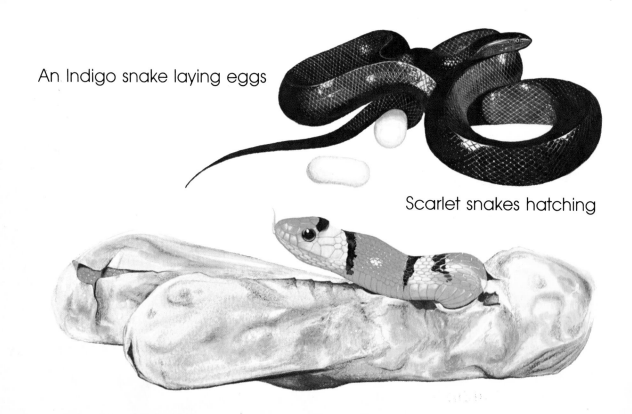

Scarlet snakes hatching

Crocodiles and alligators lay their eggs in nests that they guard carefully. When they hatch, the babies travel safely in their parents' mouths to a quiet part of the river. They can catch small creatures for themselves with their tiny sharp teeth.

A baby alligator hatching

The alligator guards her nest

Lizards

There are many different sorts of lizards.
Some of them are very pretty. Brightly colored
ones like the Gilas are often poisonous.

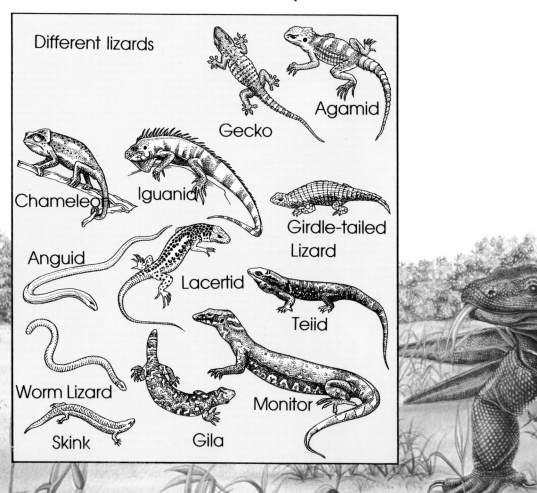

Different lizards

Gecko

Agamid

Chameleon

Iguanid

Girdle-tailed
Lizard

Anguid

Lacertid

Teiid

Worm Lizard

Monitor

Skink

Gila

Monitors are bigger than other lizards.
The Komodo Dragon of the South Pacific
Islands is the largest monitor of all.
It can grow to a length of 9½ feet (3m).
Komodo Dragons feed on animals that
are already dead or dying. They
have been known to eat their own young.

Unusual lizards

Chameleons are found in tropical forests.
They can change color to blend in with their
surroundings, so they lie in wait for
their prey without being noticed.
They catch insects with a flick of their
sticky tongues. Like all snakes and lizards,
chameleons shed their old skins regularly.

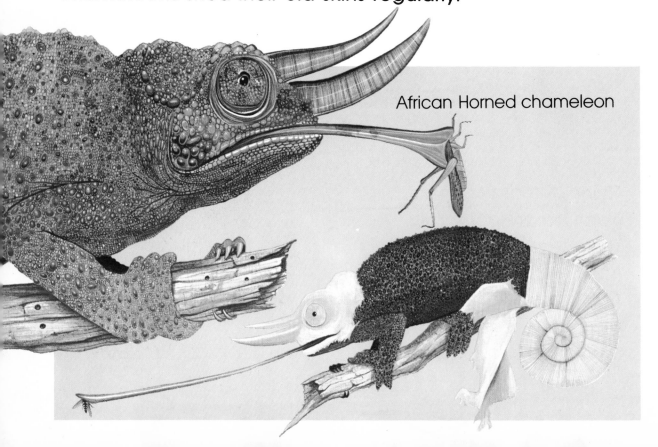

African Horned chameleon

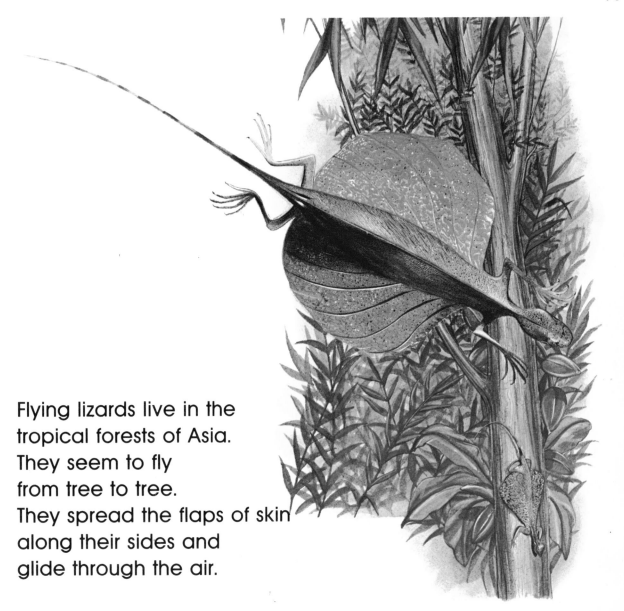

Flying lizards live in the
tropical forests of Asia.
They seem to fly
from tree to tree.
They spread the flaps of skin
along their sides and
glide through the air.

Boomslang

Snakes

Snakes are closely related to lizards but they have no legs.

Broader scales along their stomachs give extra grip as they push themselves along. Snakes flick their tongues to pick up scents.

They eat their victims whole.

They can swallow large creatures easily because their jaws are hinged to open wide.

A snake swallowing a frog

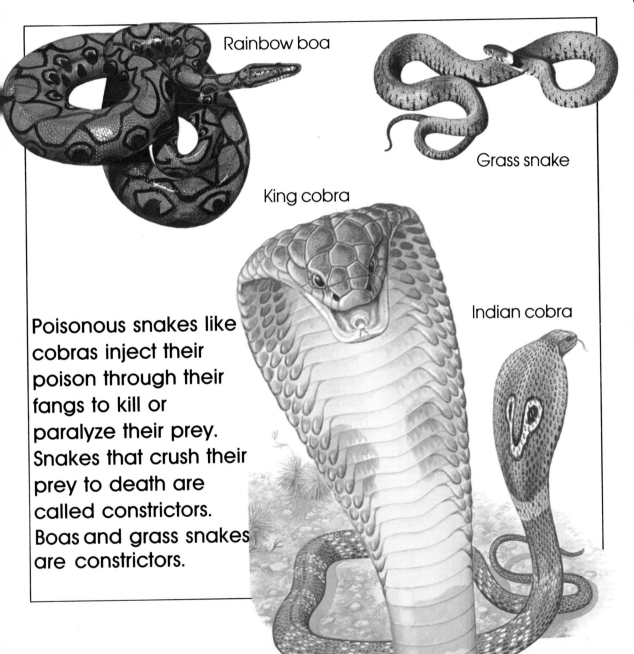

Rainbow boa

Grass snake

King cobra

Indian cobra

Poisonous snakes like cobras inject their poison through their fangs to kill or paralyze their prey. Snakes that crush their prey to death are called constrictors. Boas and grass snakes are constrictors.

Viper

Vipers

Vipers are poisonous snakes with very long fangs at the front of their mouths. The fangs fold in when the snake's mouth is closed.
There are many sorts of vipers. Rattlesnakes are vipers.

The rattle is at the end of the tail. The snake shakes it to warn enemies to keep away. It strikes very quickly.

Rattlesnake

Adders can survive in colder temperatures than most snakes. Some live in northern Europe. They will only bite a human in self defense.

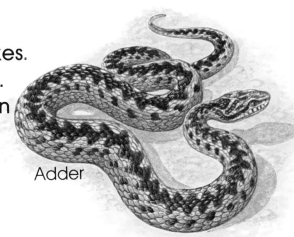

Adder

Gaboon viper

The Gaboon viper from West Africa is very dangerous. Its fangs are 2 inches (4.5cm) long. It is hard to see it hiding in the leaves.

Constrictors

Some of the biggest snakes are constrictors. Pythons and anacondas can grow up to 20 feet (6m) long. They can swim and climb trees and move along on the ground as well.

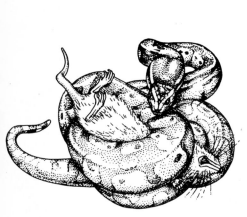

Python swimming

Crocodiles and alligators

Crocodiles, alligators and their
relations are very ancient reptiles.
They were around when
the dinosaurs were alive.
They grow very slowly but they can
be up to 20 feet (6m) long.

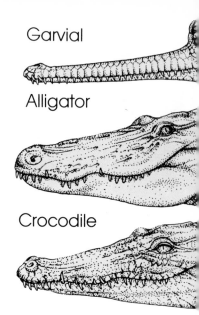

Garvial

Alligator

Crocodile

This crocodile has dragged its prey underwater.
The prey was caught when it came down
to the river to drink.
The water will soften the meat.
Crocodiles and alligators lie so still when
they are waiting for their prey that
they look like floating logs.

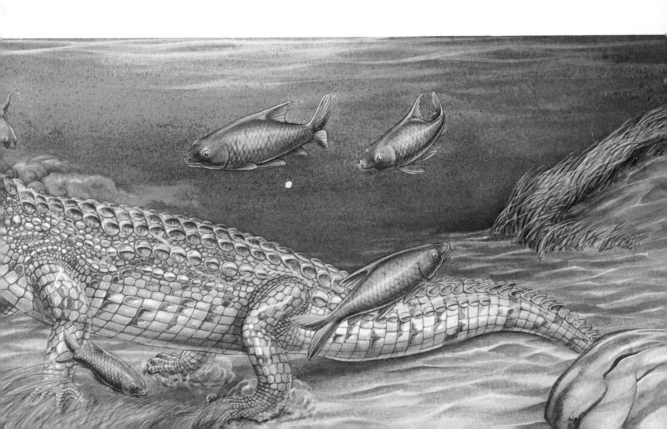

Turtles in the sea

Like all reptiles, marine turtles lay their
eggs on land. They spend the rest of their
lives in the sea. They are found in warm
oceans all over the world.

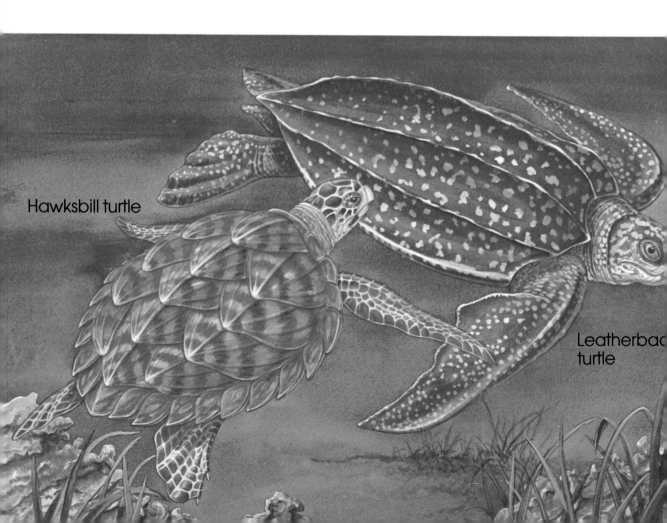

Hawksbill turtle

Leatherback
turtle

The mother turtle makes a hole in the sand for her eggs. When they hatch, the babies dig their way out of the sand and scramble down to the sea. They know how to swim right away.

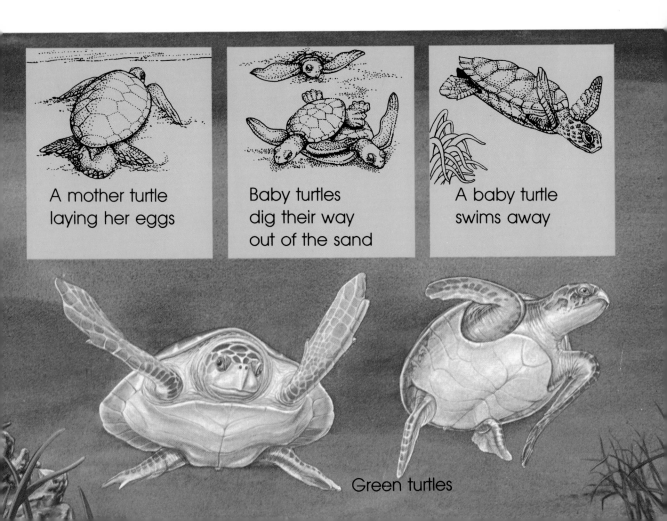

A mother turtle laying her eggs

Baby turtles dig their way out of the sand

A baby turtle swims away

Green turtles

On land and in water

Turtles have horny shells in which they can
hide. They have beak-like jaws instead of teeth.
Freshwater turtles are found in the rivers,
lakes, ponds and swamps of warm countries.

Snapper turtle

Box turtle (tortoise)

Chicker turtle

Softshell turtle

Cooter turtle

Tiny painted terrapins are sometimes kept as
pets. They need to have warm water.
The biggest turtle of all is the Giant
tortoise. It can weigh up to 350 lbs (160kg).

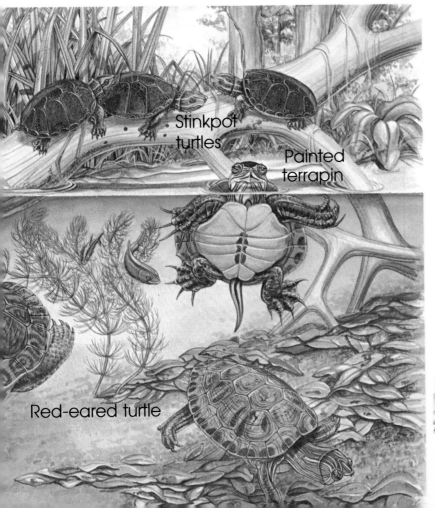

Stinkpot
turtles

Painted
terrapin

Red-eared turtle

Giant tortoise

The oldest animals in the world
There have been reptiles on Earth for over
300 million years. Some of them have changed
very little since the age of the dinosaurs.
Reptiles are not treated kindly by humans
who want their skins or their shells, or
who are simply afraid of them. It
is important for us to understand about
reptiles if we care about their survival.

Index

PRINTED IN BELGIUM BY
proost
INTERNATIONAL BOOK PRODUCTION